A Gift For: *Mary*

From: *The Delgrens*
with Love

12/05
"one"
"over"
another!

Pets' Letters to GOD

Translated By Mark Bricklin

BOK5090

This edition published in 2003 under license from Rodale Inc. exclusively for Hallmark Cards, Inc.

www.Hallmark.com

Printed and bound in China.

Cover and Interior Designer: Joanna Reinhart
Cover and Interior Illustrator: Scott Rosenkranz

2 4 6 8 10 9 7 5 3 1   hardcover

Introduction

Because we humans are not smart enough to learn the language of animals, many of us foolishly assume that they *have* no language. Or that they cannot think, reflect, question, or chuckle—let alone pray.

Actually, the reverse is true. A dog can learn the meanings of 30 or 40 human words and dozens of hand signals, not to mention body language. Yet we humans cannot master a single "word" framed in the native languages of animals! (Except "I need to go out!") So who is the better communicator? And who are we to think that animals cannot or do not communicate with God?

Our pets, who share meals, moods, even a bed *with a dominant different species*, must have profound questions about all the distressing, comforting, contradictory, and joyful things that come their way. And, no doubt, they seek answers, reassurance, and solace, just as we do.

Put yourself in their place. Reflect. Listen. Open your imagination. Do this, and you will surely be able to hear their messages to the Divine, as I have tried to do in this book.

In celebration of the bond,

Dear God,

Thank you for the ~~18~~ kittens, but you don't have to try so hard.

~Mitsy

Dear God,

Could you explain again why dogs are not allowed on a Greyhound bus?

~Tyler

Dear God,

Do bird angels have two sets of wings or is the one enough?

~Coco

Dear God,

When my family sits down to dinner, they always bless their food. But they never bless my dinner for some reason. I have the feeling I'm missing something here.

So, I've been wagging my tail extra fast when they pour out my food, as my own blessing.

Have you noticed?

~Royce

Dear God,

Do you have any pets?

Or are we all your pets?

    Love,
    Esther

Dear God,

Are hamsters permitted to reproduce in Heaven? We don't take up much room, you know!

~Binkie

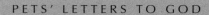

Dear God,

Is thunder absolutely necessary?

~McGwire

Dear God,

My special wish is to go to the zoo and smell all of the animals, except the snakes.

~PeeWee

Dear God,

How come people love to smell flowers, but seldom, if ever, smell one another?

Where are their priorities?

Frankly dismayed,
Turbo

Dear God,

Pardon me, but the stereo is way too loud in this house! Maybe it's my super-sensitive hearing, but nearly everything sounds like the Red Army Choir performing rap music. Once, my man put on some humpback whale songs, and I just about croaked!

Please send him some Paul Simon records.

Thank you,
Goldie

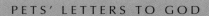

Dear God,

Is there really a food called "moused potatoes" or is this just another myth?

~Kim

Dear God,

Are there really "killer whales," or is this a figment of goldfish imagination?

~Lawanda

Dear God,

Why did it take humans 7,000 years to invent the elevated feeding bowl?

Is this rocket science?

Wondering,
Sheba

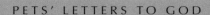

Dear God,

Does Heaven have a scent?
Sometimes I think I smell it!

~Robin

Dear God,

When we get to Heaven, can we sit on your couch?

Or is it the same old story?

~Laddie Boy

Dear God,

The new terrier I live with just pee-peed on the Turkish prayer rug! I have a feeling my family thinks I'm jealous of this stupid dog, and they might blame me! Since they have no sense of smell, how can I convince them I'm innocent?

Does PetsMart sell lie detectors?

Anxiously,
Samantha

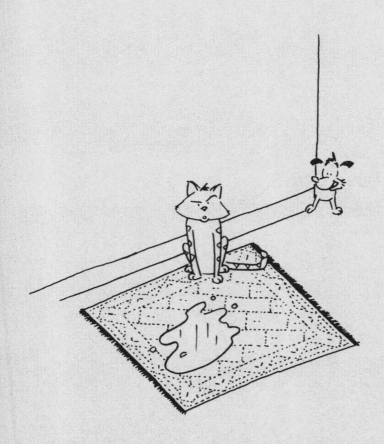

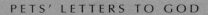

Dear God,

Must I bark, or can you hear my thoughts?

~Flo-jo

Dear God,

Are tigers really huge cats, or are cats tiny tigers?

Zenfully,
Pasha

Dear God,

Tonight, I'd like an appetizer of scallops with bacon, a small bowl of clam chowder, poached Dover sole (or Chilean sea bass, if it's fresher), and for dessert, catnip cheesecake.

Thank you for permitting me this visualization exercise.

Your friend,
Fiona

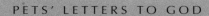

Dear God,

If books had different smells on every page, then we dogs could read, too! I've already written my first book. Here's an outline of the plot.

Chapter I: Bacon
Chapter II: Liver
Chapter III: Brie with Bacon and Liver
Chapter IV: Mommy's Pink Slippers
Chapter V: Timmy's Underwear
Chapter VI: Puppies

Could you be my agent?

Love,
Danielle

Dear God,

Excuse me, but why are there cars named after the jaguar, the cougar, the mustang, the colt, the stingray—even the rabbit!—but not a single car named for a dog?

After all, how often do you see a cougar riding around in a car? Yet we dogs love a nice ride!

I realize that every breed can't have its own model. I would suggest, though, that it would be easy and logical to rename the Chrysler Eagle the Chrysler Beagle!

Respectfully submitted,
Buford

Dear God,

Is it true that in purgatory there are 10 million cashmere sofas with porcupines sleeping on them?

~Shannon

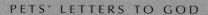

Dear God,

If a dog barks his head off in the forest, and no human hears him, is he still a bad dog?

~Butch the Boxer

Dear God,

My human has taken it into his head to make me sit still and practically beg for every morsel of dinner, which he slowly hand-feeds me.

Did he learn this at some weirdo restaurant?

~Ranger

Dear God,

Thank you for not letting cats fly!

~Mike

Dear God,

When my mommy's new friend comes over to our house in the evening, he smells like <u>musk!</u>

What's he been rolling around in?

~Ginger

Dear God,

Is Camembert cheese dead, or just really sick?

~Teddy

Dear God,

Why do I have to share my aquarium with a catfish? Is this somebody's idea of a joke?

~Maddie

Dear God,

Is it true that in Heaven, dining room tables have on-ramps?

~Trudy

Dear God,

Is it true that dogs are not permitted in restaurants because they can't make up their minds what <u>not</u> to order? Or is it the carpets again?

~Maxie

Dear God,

When I go to Heaven, will I be allowed to stick my head over the side of my cloud?

~Big Red

Dear God,

Did you create humans before you thought of color?

~Trigger

Dear God,

Is it true that dogs don't have to go to confession because priests don't have the patience to listen to all of our sins?

 Regards,
 Raptor

Dear God,

Yesterday I escaped from my cage, and now I'm in something called a closet. Is this another galaxy, a parallel universe, or what?

Confused,
André

Dear God,

If we come back as humans,
is that good or bad?

~Carla

Dear God,

I like to be scratched behind the ears.

Who scratches you?

> I love you,
> Tobi

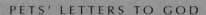

Dear God,

More meatballs, less spaghetti.

> Just a thought,
> Red Beard

Dear God,

Why don't people sleep a normal 16 hours a day?

Or does watching TV do the same thing for them?

~Caitlin

Dear God,

Please pass this message along to my so-called master:

Why are you trying to teach me to roll over and play dead? Do you find that funny? Funny <u>how</u>?

~Joe, one of your members

Dear God,

Is a bagpipe an animal?

~Robbie

Dear God,

<u>Re: Complaints about barking</u>

We dogs can understand human verbal instructions, hand signals, whistles, horns, clickers, beepers, scent IDs, electromagnetic energy fields, and Frisbee flight paths.

What do humans understand?

I rest my case.

~Rags

Dear God,

When we get to the Pearly Gates, do we have to shake hands to get in?

~Porsche

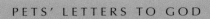

Dear God,

Is it a sin to escape from your cage?

~Roddy

Dear God,

Do we get any credit for not smoking and drinking?

~Shemp

Dear God,

Do people know that we pray, too?

Or is that just between us?

~Jax

Dear God,

Every night, a coyote comes sniffing around our house. It is quite frightening. Please give me the address of the Acme Dynamite Company.

Thank you,
Sugar

Dear God,

When I get to Heaven, can I play Frisbee with my halo?

~Nicky

Dear God,

Is the Mormon Tomcat Choir out of the question?

~Cappy

Dear God,

One thing I like is that you never interrupt when I'm talking to you!

    Worshipfully,
    Molly

Dear God,

<u>Dog</u> spelled backwards is "God."

<u>Cat</u> spelled backwards is "Tac."

Excuse me?

~Felix

Dear God,

Did you forget to create dognip?

~Kahuna

Dear God,

Are there dogs on other planets, or are we alone?

I have been howling at the moon and stars for a long time, but all I ever hear back is the beagle across the street!

~Max

Dear God,

I've always lived in the shelter, and I have everything I need. But many of the other cats here have names, and I don't.

Could you give me a name, please? It would be good for my self-esteem.

Thank you,
No-Name

Dear God,

Where does kibble come from?

And what are bits?

Bits of <u>what</u>?

    Curious,
    Maynard

Dear God,

Please ask Martha Stewart to include this tip in her magazine:

"Next Thanksgiving, when you're enjoying your turkey, why not serve your cat his own roasted quail, delicately stuffed with pan-seared jumbo Panamanian shrimp and surrounded by rosettes of foie gras nestled on little cups of catnip leaves, fresh-picked from the cold-frame herb garden I told you how to build last month. Your cat so richly deserves it!"

~Shoshana

Dear God,

Please ask Martha Stewart to include <u>this</u> tip in her magazine:

"Next Thanksgiving, why not put your cat out for a breath of fresh air, then take your turkey, put it in the blender, bones and all, and mince for 10 seconds with the top off. Next, graciously invite your dog in for a holiday dinner he'll never forget! Then, let the cat back in the house and suggest that he sniff the kitchen floor."

~Choctaw

Dear God,

I'm trying to start a business association of Really Big Animals. Could you please connect me with a grizzly bear, a rhinoceros, a Komodo dragon, a giraffe, a gorilla, and an anaconda? Also, please connect me with the World Wrestling Federation.

> Entrepreneurially yours,
> Baron,
> the Bernese Business Dog

Dear God,

I've heard that we cats have nine lives. I think I'm still on my first, but it's difficult to be sure.

Will there be a buzzer or something to let me know when I get to number eight?

~Dollee

Dear God,

Are there mailmen in Heaven?

If there are, will I have to apologize?

~Pete the Pit Bull

Dear God,

Should I tell my human that I ate her wedding ring? Or would that be in incredibly bad taste?

Repentant and confused,
Salamanca

Dear God,

We look through the windows and see all those dogs, cats, birds, and even hamsters and mice enjoying the easy life.

How do we get on family assistance, too?

>Tired of scrambling,
>Chaz Chipmunk

Dear God,

Are there hamster angels? Or am I dreaming?

~Bear

Dear God Almighty,

I am an ordained minister in the Church of Cats, 12-Nap Order. We have worked out a new service that we want to run by you:

Thank you for my home.
Thank you for my human.
Thank you for the can opener.
Thank you for the fish.
Thank you for the boat.*
Thank you for the ocean.*

Does anything come after that, or does this just about cover it?

~The Right Rev. Rosebud

*We saw this on TV.

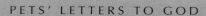

Dear God,

Hell: A million vacuum cleaners run by great big cats.

Am I close?

~Amelia

Dear God,

How do I get rid of dog breath?

~Delilah

Dear God,

Are humans on uppers, or are we on tranquilizers?

~Buddy Box Turtle

Dear God,

The other day, my main man came home, rolled up his sleeve, and showed me a big tattoo of a dog on his arm. It looks a lot like me. Under the picture are the words <u>Semper Fi</u>.

I would like to get a tattoo of him on my shoulder, with the words <u>Semper Fi, Too</u>, even though I'm not sure what those first two words mean.

However, I have no money. Do tattoo parlors accept rawhide?

> "Semper Fi,"
> Rusty

90